Naked With My Heart

PRAYER JOURNAL

Ariston C.M.

Published by Midnight Fire Industries Inc

JUST FOR YOU

THIS PRAYER JOURNAL IS MY GIFT TO YOU! IT WILL BLESS YOU IN UNEXPECTED WAYS. THIS JOURNAL IS DESIGNED TO TRACK YOUR PRAYERS. IT HAS HIDDEN GEMS, INSPIRATION, PRAYERS AND THOUGHT-PROVOKING QUESTIONS ALONG THE WAY. EACH PRAYER REQUEST SHOULD BE DATED WHEN IT WAS WRITTEN. YOU CAN WRITE YOUR PRAYERS AS OFTEN YOU WANT. BE SURE TO CHECK BACK ON YOUR PRAYERS FROM TIME TO TIME, TO SEE IF GOD HAS ANSWERED THEM. THERE IS A PLACE WHERE YOU CAN CIRCLE IF GOD HAS ANSWERED YOUR PRAYER AND THE DATE IN WHICH HE DID. DON'T BE DISCOURAGED IF YOU DON'T SEE RESULTS RIGHT AWAY, SOME PRAYERS TAKE LONGER THAN OTHERS. HE IS NEAR AND HE SEES AND HEARS YOUR HEART. I WANT TO ENCOURAGE YOU THAT WHATEVER YOU ARE BELIEVING GOD FOR, CAN HAPPEN. YOU JUST NEED TO BELIEVE. IM SURE YOU WILL BE BLESSED!!!!

IT IS WHEN WE COME TO GOD NAKED, WITH A HEAVY HEART, READY TO SURRENDER THAT HE CAN WORK BEST. AT THE POINT WHEN WE HAVE REACHED THE END OF OURSELVES, WE FIND OURSELVES IN NEED OF SOMETHING EXTRAORDINARY. IT IS AT THIS MOMENT THAT WE RELINQUISH THE RIGHTS OF OUR LIFE IN EXCHANGE FOR HIM. REGARDLESS OF YOUR BELIEFS, YOU HAVE ASKED FOR HELP FROM SOMEONE OR PERHAPS SOMETHING.

"Trust in the LORD with all your heart and lean not on your own understanding" Prov 3:5 NIV

PRAYER...

LORD, AS I BEGIN THIS JOURNEY, HELP ME UNDERSTAND YOUR PLAN FOR MY LIFE. HELP ME GAIN A GREATER UNDERSTANDING OF WHO YOU ARE. HELP ME TO BE THE PERSON YOU HAVE CALLED ME TO BE. BE MY GUIDE IN THE DARK PLACES OF MY LIFE. HEAL MY BROKENNESS, SO THAT I CAN BE FREE. OPEN MY EYES, SO THAT I CAN SEE. PROTECT MY MIND AND HEART FROM THE ENEMY. FIGHT FOR ME AND LOVE ME EVER SO DEEPLY.

AMEN!

"Come to me, all you who are weary and burdened, and I will give you rest." Matt 11:28 NIV

WHAT DO YOU NEED FROM GOD?

This is the time to be transparent...It's just you and God (He sees you)

"Trust in the LORD with all your heart and lean not on your own understanding" Prov 3:5 NIV

PRAYER

Date: ______ Mood: ______

______

______

______

______ Prayer Answered? Yes or No Date ______

PRAYER

Date: ______ Mood: ______

______

______

______

______ Prayer Answered? Yes or No Date ______

PRAYER

Date: ______ Mood: ______

______

______

______

______ Prayer Answered? Yes or No Date ______

"Come to me, all you who are weary and burdened, and I will give you rest." Matt 11:28 NIV

PRAYER

Date: ______________ Mood: ______________

Prayer Answered? Yes or No Date ______

PRAYER

Date: ______________ Mood: ______________

Prayer Answered? Yes or No Date ______

PRAYER

Date: ______________ Mood: ______________

Prayer Answered? Yes or No Date ______

"Trust in the LORD with all your heart and lean not on your own understanding" Prov 3:5 NIV

PRAYER

Date: ______________ Mood: ______________

Prayer Answered? Yes or No Date ______

PRAYER

Date: ______________ Mood: ______________

Prayer Answered? Yes or No Date ______

PRAYER

Date: ______________ Mood: ______________

Prayer Answered? Yes or No Date ______

"Come to me, all you who are weary and burdened, and I will give you rest." Matt 11:28 NIV

PRAYER

Date: ____________ Mood: ____________

Prayer Answered? Yes or No Date ______

PRAYER

Date: ____________ Mood: ____________

Prayer Answered? Yes or No Date ______

PRAYER

Date: ____________ Mood: ____________

Prayer Answered? Yes or No Date ______

"Trust in the LORD with all your heart and lean not on your own understanding" Prov 3:5 NIV

THOUGHTS

"Come to me, all you who are weary and burdened, and I will give you rest." Matt 11:28 NIV

PRAYER

Date: __________ Mood: __________

Prayer Answered? Yes or No Date

PRAYER

Date: __________ Mood: __________

Prayer Answered? Yes or No Date

PRAYER

Date: __________ Mood: __________

Prayer Answered? Yes or No Date

"Trust in the LORD with all your heart and lean not on your own understanding" Prov 3:5 NIV

PRAYER

Date: ______________ Mood: ______________

Prayer Answered? Yes or No Date ______

PRAYER

Date: ______________ Mood: ______________

Prayer Answered? Yes or No Date ______

PRAYER

Date: ______________ Mood: ______________

Prayer Answered? Yes or No Date ______

"Come to me, all you who are weary and burdened, and I will give you rest." Matt 11:28 NIV

PRAYER

Date: ______________ Mood: ______________

____

____

____

______________ Prayer Answered? Yes or No Date ______

PRAYER

Date: ______________ Mood: ______________

____

____

____

______________ Prayer Answered? Yes or No Date ______

PRAYER

Date: ______________ Mood: ______________

____

____

____

______________ Prayer Answered? Yes or No Date ______

"Trust in the LORD with all your heart and lean not on your own understanding" Prov 3:5 NIV

PRAYER

Date: ______________ Mood: ______________

Prayer Answered? Yes or No Date ______

PRAYER

Date: ______________ Mood: ______________

Prayer Answered? Yes or No Date ______

PRAYER

Date: ______________ Mood: ______________

Prayer Answered? Yes or No Date ______

"Come to me, all you who are weary and burdened, and I will give you rest." Matt 11:28 NIV

GETTING TO KNOW THE REAL YOU

Strength

"Your greatest strength lies in your ability to draw power from the same source, that drives your weaknesses allowing them manifest into strength."

-Ariston CM

Weaknesses

"Trust in the LORD with all your heart and lean not on your own understanding" Prov 3:5 NIV

PRAYER...

LORD I COME TO YOU, IMPERFECT WITH DIFFERENT SHADES OF FLAWS. I MAY EVEN HIDE BEHIND DIFFERENT FACES, SO MY WEAKNESS DOESN'T SHOW AT ALL. I ASK YOU TO BE MY STRENGTH, SO THAT I'M NOT TEMPTED LET GO. HELP ME TO UNDERSTAND BY ACKNOWLEDGING MY WEAKNESS, THIS WILL GIVE ME THE POWER TO GROW. BE MY GUIDE IN THE DARK MOMENTS OF MY LIFE. SHIELD ME AND PROTECT ME, LIGHT MY PATH, SO I DON'T GET LOST IN THE NIGHT. TOUCH ME IN A WAY THAT I CAN FEEL. HOLD ME CLOSE, I NEED TO KNOW YOUR LOVE IS REAL...

AMEN!

"Come to me, all you who are weary and burdened, and I will give you rest." Matt 11:28 NIV

THOUGHTS

"Trust in the LORD with all your heart and lean not on your own understanding" Prov 3:5 NIV

IT'S ONLY UP FROM HERE

Goal completed? Yes or No Date

Goals

Goal completed? Yes or No Date

"Come to me, all you who are weary and burdened, and I will give you rest." Matt 11:28 NIV

PRAYER

Date: ____________ Mood: ____________

Prayer Answered? Yes or No Date ________

PRAYER

Date: ____________ Mood: ____________

Prayer Answered? Yes or No Date ________

PRAYER

Date: ____________ Mood: ____________

Prayer Answered? Yes or No Date ________

"Trust in the LORD with all your heart and lean not on your own understanding" Prov 3:5 NIV

PRAYER

Date: ______ Mood: ______

Prayer Answered? Yes or No Date ______

PRAYER

Date: ______ Mood: ______

Prayer Answered? Yes or No Date ______

PRAYER

Date: ______ Mood: ______

Prayer Answered? Yes or No Date ______

"Come to me, all you who are weary and burdened, and I will give you rest." Matt 11:28 NIV

PRAYER

Date: ______________________ Mood: ______________________

____

____

____

______________________ Prayer Answered? Yes or No Date __________

PRAYER

Date: ______________________ Mood: ______________________

____

____

____

______________________ Prayer Answered? Yes or No Date __________

PRAYER

Date: ______________________ Mood: ______________________

____

____

____

______________________ Prayer Answered? Yes or No Date __________

"Trust in the LORD with all your heart and lean not on your own understanding" Prov 3:5 NIV

PRAYER

Date: Mood:

Prayer Answered? Yes or No Date

PRAYER

Date: Mood:

Prayer Answered? Yes or No Date

PRAYER

Date: Mood:

Prayer Answered? Yes or No Date

"Come to me, all you who are weary and burdened, and I will give you rest." Matt 11:28 NIV

“

Beautiful Soul, You Deserve more than anything to be loved, fulfilled and adorned with purpose.

-Ariston CM

PRAYER

Date: ______ Mood: ______

______

______

______

______ Prayer Answered? Yes or No Date ______

PRAYER

Date: ______ Mood: ______

______

______

______

______ Prayer Answered? Yes or No Date ______

PRAYER

Date: ______ Mood: ______

______

______

______

______ Prayer Answered? Yes or No Date ______

"Come to me, all you who are weary and burdened, and I will give you rest." Matt 11:28 NIV

PRAYER

Date: ______________ Mood: ______________

____

____

____

______________ Prayer Answered? Yes or No Date ______

PRAYER

Date: ______________ Mood: ______________

____

____

____

______________ Prayer Answered? Yes or No Date ______

PRAYER

Date: ______________ Mood: ______________

____

____

____

______________ Prayer Answered? Yes or No Date ______

"Trust in the LORD with all your heart and lean not on your own understanding" Prov 3:5 NIV

PRAYER

Date: ______________ Mood: ______________

Prayer Answered? Yes or No Date

PRAYER

Date: ______________ Mood: ______________

Prayer Answered? Yes or No Date

PRAYER

Date: ______________ Mood: ______________

Prayer Answered? Yes or No Date

"Come to me, all you who are weary and burdened, and I will give you rest." Matt 11:28 NIV

FEAR NOT

I HAVE CALLED YOU BY NAME

FEAR PLANTS DOUBT...WRITE IT OUT LET'S UPROOT IT

"Trust in the LORD with all your heart and lean not on your own understanding" Prov 3:5 NIV

PRAYER

Date: ____________ Mood: ____________

Prayer Answered? Yes or No Date ______

PRAYER

Date: ____________ Mood: ____________

Prayer Answered? Yes or No Date ______

PRAYER

Date: ____________ Mood: ____________

Prayer Answered? Yes or No Date ______

"Come to me, all you who are weary and burdened, and I will give you rest." Matt 11:28 NIV

PRAYER

Date: ____________ Mood: ____________

____

____

____

____________ Prayer Answered? Yes or No Date ________

PRAYER

Date: ____________ Mood: ____________

____

____

____

____________ Prayer Answered? Yes or No Date ________

PRAYER

Date: ____________ Mood: ____________

____

____

____

____________ Prayer Answered? Yes or No Date ________

"Trust in the LORD with all your heart and lean not on your own understanding" Prov 3:5 NIV

PRAYER

Date: ______________ Mood: ______________

____

____

____

______________ Prayer Answered? Yes or No Date ______

PRAYER

Date: ______________ Mood: ______________

____

____

____

______________ Prayer Answered? Yes or No Date ______

PRAYER

Date: ______________ Mood: ______________

____

____

____

______________ Prayer Answered? Yes or No Date ______

"Come to me, all you who are weary and burdened, and I will give you rest." Matt 11:28 NIV

PRAYER

Date: ____________ Mood: ____________

Prayer Answered? Yes or No Date ________

PRAYER

Date: ____________ Mood: ____________

Prayer Answered? Yes or No Date ________

PRAYER

Date: ____________ Mood: ____________

Prayer Answered? Yes or No Date ________

"Trust in the LORD with all your heart and lean not on your own understanding" Prov 3:5 NIV

PRAYER

Date: ______________ Mood: ______________

____

____

____

______________ Prayer Answered? Yes or No Date ______

PRAYER

Date: ______________ Mood: ______________

____

____

____

______________ Prayer Answered? Yes or No Date ______

PRAYER

Date: ______________ Mood: ______________

____

____

____

______________ Prayer Answered? Yes or No Date ______

"Come to me, all you who are weary and burdened, and I will give you rest." Matt 11:28 NIV

PRAYER

Date: ______________ Mood: ______________

____

____

____

______________ Prayer Answered? Yes or No Date ________

PRAYER

Date: ______________ Mood: ______________

____

____

____

______________ Prayer Answered? Yes or No Date ________

PRAYER

Date: ______________ Mood: ______________

____

____

____

______________ Prayer Answered? Yes or No Date ________

"Trust in the LORD with all your heart and lean not on your own understanding" Prov 3:5 NIV

PRAYER

Date: ______________ Mood: ______________

Prayer Answered? Yes or No Date

PRAYER

Date: ______________ Mood: ______________

Prayer Answered? Yes or No Date

PRAYER

Date: ______________ Mood: ______________

Prayer Answered? Yes or No Date

"Come to me, all you who are weary and burdened, and I will give you rest." Matt 11:28 NIV

DATE NIGHT WITH THE KING

Just like you would nurture your relationship with your child, significant other, close friend or family member; you must do the same with God. Be intentional and set time apart for Him. He wants you; He desires to be in relationship with you. Its okay to be creative, no need to box God in or put limits on Him. Get comfy and cozy, He is God!

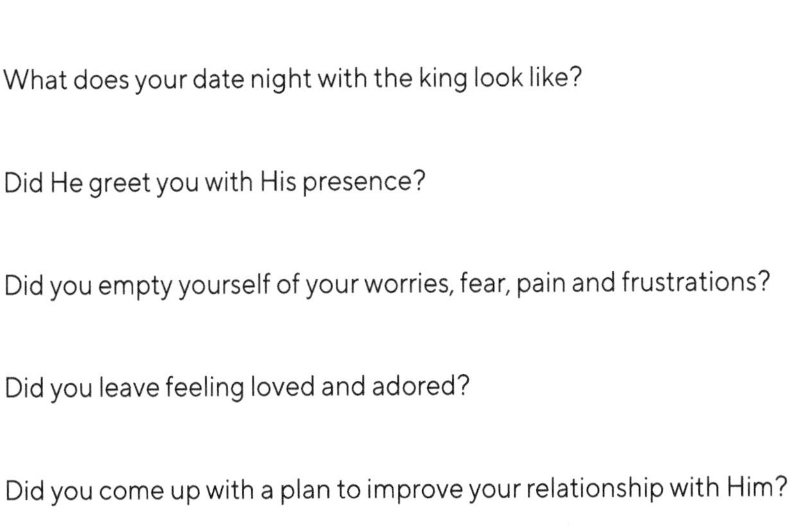

What does your date night with the king look like?

Did He greet you with His presence?

Did you empty yourself of your worries, fear, pain and frustrations?

Did you leave feeling loved and adored?

Did you come up with a plan to improve your relationship with Him?

"Trust in the LORD with all your heart and lean not on your own understanding" Prov 3:5 NIV

NAKED THOUGHTS

- He Wants It All -

Don't you feel much better? You should, you deserve to be free...

"Come to me, all you who are weary and burdened, and I will give you rest." Matt 11:28 NIV

PRAYER

Date: ______________ Mood: ______________

Prayer Answered? Yes or No Date ______

PRAYER

Date: ______________ Mood: ______________

Prayer Answered? Yes or No Date ______

PRAYER

Date: ______________ Mood: ______________

Prayer Answered? Yes or No Date ______

"Trust in the LORD with all your heart and lean not on your own understanding" Prov 3:5 NIV

PRAYER

Date: ________________ Mood: ________________

Prayer Answered? Yes or No Date

PRAYER

Date: ________________ Mood: ________________

Prayer Answered? Yes or No Date

PRAYER

Date: ________________ Mood: ________________

Prayer Answered? Yes or No Date

"Come to me, all you who are weary and burdened, and I will give you rest." Matt 11:28 NIV

PRAYER

Date: ______________ Mood: ______________

____

____

____

______________ Prayer Answered? Yes or No Date ______

PRAYER

Date: ______________ Mood: ______________

____

____

____

______________ Prayer Answered? Yes or No Date ______

PRAYER

Date: ______________ Mood: ______________

____

____

____

______________ Prayer Answered? Yes or No Date ______

"Trust in the LORD with all your heart and lean not on your own understanding" Prov 3:5 NIV

PRAYER

Date: ____________ Mood: ____________

Prayer Answered? Yes or No Date ________

PRAYER

Date: ____________ Mood: ____________

Prayer Answered? Yes or No Date ________

PRAYER

Date: ____________ Mood: ____________

Prayer Answered? Yes or No Date ________

"Come to me, all you who are weary and burdened, and I will give you rest." Matt 11:28 NIV

PRAYER

Date: ________________ Mood: ________________

Prayer Answered? Yes or No Date

PRAYER

Date: ________________ Mood: ________________

Prayer Answered? Yes or No Date

PRAYER

Date: ________________ Mood: ________________

Prayer Answered? Yes or No Date

"Trust in the LORD with all your heart and lean not on your own understanding" Prov 3:5 NIV

PRAYER

Date: ______________ Mood: ______________

Prayer Answered? Yes or No Date ______

PRAYER

Date: ______________ Mood: ______________

Prayer Answered? Yes or No Date ______

PRAYER

Date: ______________ Mood: ______________

Prayer Answered? Yes or No Date ______

"Come to me, all you who are weary and burdened, and I will give you rest." Matt 11:28 NIV

IT'S YOUR TIME TO SHINE

Self-love is the best love…Let's hear it

Positive Affirmations

"Trust in the LORD with all your heart and lean not on your own understanding" Prov 3:5 NIV

PRAYER

Date: ______________ Mood: ______________

Prayer Answered? Yes or No Date ______

PRAYER

Date: ______________ Mood: ______________

Prayer Answered? Yes or No Date ______

PRAYER

Date: ______________ Mood: ______________

Prayer Answered? Yes or No Date ______

"Come to me, all you who are weary and burdened, and I will give you rest." Matt 11:28 NIV

PRAYER

Date: __________ Mood: __________

__________ Prayer Answered? Yes or No Date __________

PRAYER

Date: __________ Mood: __________

__________ Prayer Answered? Yes or No Date __________

PRAYER

Date: __________ Mood: __________

__________ Prayer Answered? Yes or No Date __________

"Trust in the LORD with all your heart and lean not on your own understanding" Prov 3:5 NIV

PRAYER

Date: ______________ Mood: ______________

Prayer Answered? Yes or No Date ______

PRAYER

Date: ______________ Mood: ______________

Prayer Answered? Yes or No Date ______

PRAYER

Date: ______________ Mood: ______________

Prayer Answered? Yes or No Date ______

"Come to me, all you who are weary and burdened, and I will give you rest." Matt 11:28 NIV

PRAYER

Date: ______________ Mood: ______________

Prayer Answered? Yes or No Date

PRAYER

Date: ______________ Mood: ______________

Prayer Answered? Yes or No Date

PRAYER

Date: ______________ Mood: ______________

Prayer Answered? Yes or No Date

"Trust in the LORD with all your heart and lean not on your own understanding" Prov 3:5 NIV

PROCRASTINATION KILLS YOUR PURPOSE

List Some Ways You Procrastinate

1. ______________________________

2. ______________________________

3. ______________________________

4. ______________________________

5. ______________________________

Sooo how are you going to change this? Think About it.

"Come to me, all you who are weary and burdened, and I will give you rest." Matt 11:28 NIV

PRAYER

Date: ____________ Mood: ____________

Prayer Answered? Yes or No Date ______

PRAYER

Date: ____________ Mood: ____________

Prayer Answered? Yes or No Date ______

PRAYER

Date: ____________ Mood: ____________

Prayer Answered? Yes or No Date ______

"Trust in the LORD with all your heart and lean not on your own understanding" Prov 3:5 NIV

PRAYER

Date: ______________ Mood: ______________

____

____

____

______________ Prayer Answered? Yes or No Date ______

PRAYER

Date: ______________ Mood: ______________

____

____

____

______________ Prayer Answered? Yes or No Date ______

PRAYER

Date: ______________ Mood: ______________

____

____

____

______________ Prayer Answered? Yes or No Date ______

"Come to me, all you who are weary and burdened, and I will give you rest." Matt 11:28 NIV

PRAYER

Date: ____________ Mood: ____________

Prayer Answered? Yes or No Date ____

PRAYER

Date: ____________ Mood: ____________

Prayer Answered? Yes or No Date ____

PRAYER

Date: ____________ Mood: ____________

Prayer Answered? Yes or No Date ____

"Trust in the LORD with all your heart and lean not on your own understanding" Prov 3:5 NIV

PRAYER

Date: ____________ Mood: ____________

Prayer Answered? Yes or No Date ____________

PRAYER

Date: ____________ Mood: ____________

Prayer Answered? Yes or No Date ____________

PRAYER

Date: ____________ Mood: ____________

Prayer Answered? Yes or No Date ____________

"Come to me, all you who are weary and burdened, and I will give you rest." Matt 11:28 NIV

RAW THOUGHTS

- The First Thing That Comes To Your Mind -

It perfect to be imperfect...Honesty is the best policy

"Trust in the LORD with all your heart and lean not on your own understanding" Prov 3:5 NIV

PRAYER

Date: ______________ Mood: ______________

Prayer Answered? Yes or No Date

PRAYER

Date: ______________ Mood: ______________

Prayer Answered? Yes or No Date

PRAYER

Date: ______________ Mood: ______________

Prayer Answered? Yes or No Date

"Come to me, all you who are weary and burdened, and I will give you rest." Matt 11:28 NIV

PRAYER

Date: ______ Mood: ______

Prayer Answered? Yes or No Date ______

PRAYER

Date: ______ Mood: ______

Prayer Answered? Yes or No Date ______

PRAYER

Date: ______ Mood: ______

Prayer Answered? Yes or No Date ______

"Trust in the LORD with all your heart and lean not on your own understanding" Prov 3:5 NIV

PRAYER

Date: ______________ Mood: ______________

____

____

____

______________ Prayer Answered? Yes or No Date ______

PRAYER

Date: ______________ Mood: ______________

____

____

____

______________ Prayer Answered? Yes or No Date ______

PRAYER

Date: ______________ Mood: ______________

____

____

____

______________ Prayer Answered? Yes or No Date ______

"Come to me, all you who are weary and burdened, and I will give you rest." Matt 11:28 NIV

PRAYER

Date: ______________________ Mood: ______________________

____

____

____

______________________ Prayer Answered? Yes or No Date __________

PRAYER

Date: ______________________ Mood: ______________________

____

____

____

______________________ Prayer Answered? Yes or No Date __________

PRAYER

Date: ______________________ Mood: ______________________

____

____

____

______________________ Prayer Answered? Yes or No Date __________

"Trust in the LORD with all your heart and lean not on your own understanding" Prov 3:5 NIV

PRAYER

Date: ____________________ Mood: ____________________

____________________ Prayer Answered? Yes or No Date ____________

PRAYER

Date: ____________________ Mood: ____________________

____________________ Prayer Answered? Yes or No Date ____________

PRAYER

Date: ____________________ Mood: ____________________

____________________ Prayer Answered? Yes or No Date ____________

"Come to me, all you who are weary and burdened, and I will give you rest." Matt 11:28 NIV

REFLECTIONS

- What Have You Learned About Yourself? -

"Trust in the LORD with all your heart and lean not on your own understanding" Prov 3:5 NIV

REFLECTIONS

- What Have You Learned About God? -

"Come to me, all you who are weary and burdened, and I will give you rest." Matt 11:28 NIV

REFLECTIONS

- What Will Truly Make You Happy? -

"Trust in the LORD with all your heart and lean not on your own understanding" Prov 3:5 NIV

REFLECTIONS

- What Habit Can You Live Without? -

"Come to me, all you who are weary and burdened, and I will give you rest." Matt 11:28 NIV

RAW THOUGHTS

- What Is Your Biggest Struggle...Why? -

"Trust in the LORD with all your heart and lean not on your own understanding" Prov 3:5 NIV

RAW THOUGHTS

If You Could Be Or Do Anything In The World Without Any Limitations, What Would That Be?

"Come to me, all you who are weary and burdened, and I will give you rest." Matt 11:28 NIV

THE BLANK PAGES OF YOUR HEART

"Trust in the LORD with all your heart and lean not on your own understanding" Prov 3:5 NIV

THE BLANK PAGES OF YOUR HEART

"Come to me, all you who are weary and burdened, and I will give you rest." Matt 11:28 NIV

THE BLANK PAGES OF YOUR HEART

"Trust in the LORD with all your heart and lean not on your own understanding" Prov 3:5 NIV

THE BLANK PAGES OF YOUR HEART

"Come to me, all you who are weary and burdened, and I will give you rest." Matt 11:28 NIV

THE BLANK PAGES OF YOUR HEART

"Trust in the LORD with all your heart and lean not on your own understanding" Prov 3:5 NIV

THE BLANK PAGES OF YOUR HEART

"Come to me, all you who are weary and burdened, and I will give you rest." Matt 11:28 NIV

THE BLANK PAGES OF YOUR HEART

"Trust in the LORD with all your heart and lean not on your own understanding" Prov 3:5 NIV

THE BLANK PAGES OF YOUR HEART

"Come to me, all you who are weary and burdened, and I will give you rest." Matt 11:28 NIV

THE BLANK PAGES OF YOUR HEART

"Trust in the LORD with all your heart and lean not on your own understanding" Prov 3:5 NIV

THE BLANK PAGES OF YOUR HEART

"Come to me, all you who are weary and burdened, and I will give you rest." Matt 11:28 NIV

THE BLANK PAGES OF YOUR HEART

"Trust in the LORD with all your heart and lean not on your own understanding" Prov 3:5 NIV

THE BLANK PAGES OF YOUR HEART

"Come to me, all you who are weary and burdened, and I will give you rest." Matt 11:28 NIV

THE BLANK PAGES OF YOUR HEART

"Trust in the LORD with all your heart and lean not on your own understanding" Prov 3:5 NIV

THE BLANK PAGES OF YOUR HEART

"Come to me, all you who are weary and burdened, and I will give you rest." Matt 11:28 NIV

THE BLANK PAGES OF YOUR HEART

"Trust in the LORD with all your heart and lean not on your own understanding" Prov 3:5 NIV

THE BLANK PAGES OF YOUR HEART

"Come to me, all you who are weary and burdened, and I will give you rest." Matt 11:28 NIV

THE BLANK PAGES OF YOUR HEART

"Trust in the LORD with all your heart and lean not on your own understanding" Prov 3:5 NIV

THE BLANK PAGES OF YOUR HEART

"Come to me, all you who are weary and burdened, and I will give you rest." Matt 11:28 NIV

THE BLANK PAGES OF YOUR HEART

"Trust in the LORD with all your heart and lean not on your own understanding" Prov 3:5 NIV

THE BLANK PAGES OF YOUR HEART

"Come to me, all you who are weary and burdened, and I will give you rest." Matt 11:28 NIV

THE BLANK PAGES OF YOUR HEART

"Trust in the LORD with all your heart and lean not on your own understanding" Prov 3:5 NIV

THE BLANK PAGES OF YOUR HEART

"Come to me, all you who are weary and burdened, and I will give you rest." Matt 11:28 NIV

PROGRESS & UPDATES

"Trust in the LORD with all your heart and lean not on your own understanding" Prov 3:5 NIV

PROGRESS & UPDATES

"Come to me, all you who are weary and burdened, and I will give you rest." Matt 11:28 NIV

WHAT IS GOD DOING IN YOUR LIFE?

"Trust in the LORD with all your heart and lean not on your own understanding" Prov 3:5 NIV

WHAT IS GOD DOING IN YOUR LIFE?

"Come to me, all you who are weary and burdened, and I will give you rest." Matt 11:28 NIV

In The Beginning Of This Journal, You Wanted Something From God Did You Receive It?

"Trust in the LORD with all your heart and lean not on your own understanding" Prov 3:5 NIV

PRAYER

Date: ____________ Mood: ____________

Prayer Answered? Yes or No Date ____________

PRAYER

Date: ____________ Mood: ____________

Prayer Answered? Yes or No Date ____________

PRAYER

Date: ____________ Mood: ____________

Prayer Answered? Yes or No Date ____________

"Come to me, all you who are weary and burdened, and I will give you rest." Matt 11:28 NIV

PRAYER

Date: ____________ Mood: ____________

Prayer Answered? Yes or No Date ________

PRAYER

Date: ____________ Mood: ____________

Prayer Answered? Yes or No Date ________

PRAYER

Date: ____________ Mood: ____________

Prayer Answered? Yes or No Date ________

"Trust in the LORD with all your heart and lean not on your own understanding" Prov 3:5 NIV

PRAYER

Date: ______________________ Mood: ______________________

Prayer Answered? Yes or No Date

PRAYER

Date: ______________________ Mood: ______________________

Prayer Answered? Yes or No Date

PRAYER

Date: ______________________ Mood: ______________________

Prayer Answered? Yes or No Date

"Come to me, all you who are weary and burdened, and I will give you rest." Matt 11:28 NIV

PRAYER

Date: ______________ Mood: ______________

Prayer Answered? Yes or No Date ______

PRAYER

Date: ______________ Mood: ______________

Prayer Answered? Yes or No Date ______

PRAYER

Date: ______________ Mood: ______________

Prayer Answered? Yes or No Date ______

"Trust in the LORD with all your heart and lean not on your own understanding" Prov 3:5 NIV

PRAYER

Date: ________________ Mood: ________________

Prayer Answered? Yes or No Date ________

PRAYER

Date: ________________ Mood: ________________

Prayer Answered? Yes or No Date ________

PRAYER

Date: ________________ Mood: ________________

Prayer Answered? Yes or No Date ________

"Come to me, all you who are weary and burdened, and I will give you rest." Matt 11:28 NIV

PRAYER

Date: ______________ Mood: ______________

Prayer Answered? Yes or No Date ______

PRAYER

Date: ______________ Mood: ______________

Prayer Answered? Yes or No Date ______

PRAYER

Date: ______________ Mood: ______________

Prayer Answered? Yes or No Date ______

"Trust in the LORD with all your heart and lean not on your own understanding" Prov 3:5 NIV

PRAYER

Date: ______________ Mood: ______________

Prayer Answered? Yes or No Date

PRAYER

Date: ______________ Mood: ______________

Prayer Answered? Yes or No Date

PRAYER

Date: ______________ Mood: ______________

Prayer Answered? Yes or No Date

"Come to me, all you who are weary and burdened, and I will give you rest." Matt 11:28 NIV

PRAYER

Date: ______________ Mood: ______________

____

____

____

______________________ Prayer Answered? Yes or No Date ________

PRAYER

Date: ______________ Mood: ______________

____

____

____

______________________ Prayer Answered? Yes or No Date ________

PRAYER

Date: ______________ Mood: ______________

____

____

____

______________________ Prayer Answered? Yes or No Date ________

"Trust in the LORD with all your heart and lean not on your own understanding" Prov 3:5 NIV

PRAYER

Date: ______________ Mood: ______________

Prayer Answered? Yes or No Date ______

PRAYER

Date: ______________ Mood: ______________

Prayer Answered? Yes or No Date ______

PRAYER

Date: ______________ Mood: ______________

Prayer Answered? Yes or No Date ______

"Come to me, all you who are weary and burdened, and I will give you rest." Matt 11:28 NIV

PRAYER

Date: ____________________ Mood: ____________________

Prayer Answered? Yes or No Date

PRAYER

Date: ____________________ Mood: ____________________

Prayer Answered? Yes or No Date

PRAYER

Date: ____________________ Mood: ____________________

Prayer Answered? Yes or No Date

"Trust in the LORD with all your heart and lean not on your own understanding" Prov 3:5 NIV

PRAYER

Date: ____________ Mood: ____________

Prayer Answered? Yes or No Date ________

PRAYER

Date: ____________ Mood: ____________

Prayer Answered? Yes or No Date ________

PRAYER

Date: ____________ Mood: ____________

Prayer Answered? Yes or No Date ________

"Come to me, all you who are weary and burdened, and I will give you rest." Matt 11:28 NIV

PRAYER...

I PRAY THAT YOU HAVE BEEN STRENGTHENED IN EVERY AREA OF YOUR LIFE. YOUR WALK IS NOT GOING TO BE EASY, BUT KNOW THAT GOD WILL BLESS YOU BEYOND MEASURE. I PRAY THESE WORDS PENETRATE YOUR SOUL AND CARESS YOUR HEART. HE LONGS TO HAVE A DEEP INTIMATE RELATIONSHIP WITH YOU. CONTINUE TO TRUST HIM WITH YOUR WHOLE LIFE AND I PROMISE HE WILL TAKE CARE OF YOU. BE BLESSED AND KNOW THAT YOUR JOURNEY IS NOT IN VAIN. EVERY CROOKED PLACE WILL BE MADE STRAIGHT. I WILL BE PRAYING YOUR STRENGTH IN THE LORD.

AMEN!

The End

YOUR NEW CHAPTER AWAITS..

- love Ariston

"Come to me, all you who are weary and burdened, and I will give you rest." Matt 11:28 NIV

You Are Appreciated...

Thank you so much for purchasing my prayer journal. I Pray that it has helped you gain a closer walk with your "Creator". If you have not had the chance to get my other books; "The Courage to Dance Again" Finding purpose in your pain, "Naked With My Heart" 7 days to spiritual oneness and "Poetry's Love Song", they are available on Amazon. Get your copies today!

It would definitely make me smile if I heard from you! Connect with me, I want to hear all about your Journey! Ways to connect with me:

Email: connect@loveariston.com
Website: LoveAriston.com

Of course I'm on social media...

@Ariston CM

@imsoariston

Hugs & Kisses, Ariston!

ABOUT THE AUTHOR

Ariston C.M. was born and currently resides in Ohio. She is an entrepreneur and has a Master's in Christian Education, Diploma of Theology in Black Church Studies, Child Development Associate Credential (CDA) and working toward a second Master's in Clinical Counseling. Her challenges as a child ultimately inspired her to start a non-profit organization that currently addresses the needs of at-risk youth and those with developmental disabilities.

Ariston has developed a multitude of programs, curriculum, and taught various workshops. She is a speaker both national and international. She is passionate about empowering individuals to live beyond their pain and walk in their purpose. In her free time, she enjoys nature, traveling and spending quality time with her children. Ariston's husband is a pastor and they have a church in Ghana. Ariston has three other books, "The Courage to Dance Again" finding purpose in your pain, "Naked With My Heart" 7 days to spiritual oneness and "Poetrys Love Song". All are available on Amazon.

CPSIA information can be obtained
at www.ICGtesting.com
Printed in the USA
LVHW071447010920
664636LV00014B/747